Birthdays Around the World

Written by Lisa Weir

Contents

Birthdays	2
Birthday Cake	4
Birthday Wreath	6
Birthday Drink	8
Birthday Game	10
Birthday Meal	12
Birthday Surprise	14
Glossary	16

Birthdays

How do you **celebrate** your birthday?

Do you have a cake with candles?

Do you have a party with your family and friends?

Around the world, children celebrate their birthdays in different ways.

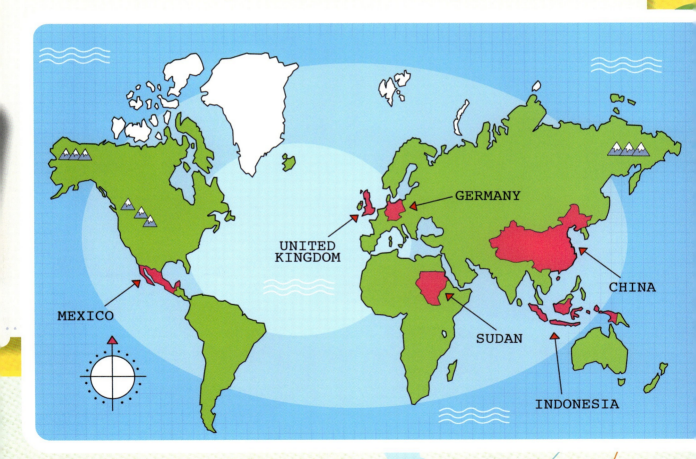

Birthday Cake

In Indonesia, some children have a birthday cake made of rice.

The rice is made into a cone shape. Food is placed around the cone.

Birthday Wreath

In Germany, some children have a **wreath** for their birthday candles.

The wreath is made from wood and holds the candles.

6

Birthday Drink

In Sudan, some children have a drink made from flowers on their birthday.

They use **hibiscus** (say *hib-iss-kuss*) flowers. The drink is red and it tastes sweet.

Birthday Game

In the UK, some children play games on their birthday.

One game is called pass-the-parcel. Children sit down. They take turns to rip off a layer of paper from the parcel.

The child to rip off the last layer keeps the present inside.

Birthday Meal

In China, some children eat eggs and noodles on their birthday.

The eggs are for good luck.
The noodles are for a long life.

Birthday Surprise

In Mexico, some children have a **piñata** (say *pin-ya-ta*) at their party.

Children hit the piñata with a stick. The piñata splits and toys or sweets fall out.

Glossary

celebrate have fun

hibiscus bright flower that grows in warm places

piñata decorated object, often in an animal shape, with toys or sweets inside

wreath decorated ring